T0303662

More Praise for
Twice Shy

Twice Shy looks violence in the face—in all its faces—and recognizes how it victimizes (the "skin he unzipped you from"), but more importantly recognizes how we "all the time, carry survival." The voices of this collection become memory, become compassion, but ultimately become animal—one whose role is to survive. It begs the question: Is radical tenderness just as much an embraceable nature of ourselves as our brutality? Radical tenderness is indeed the kind of survival that Flynn-Goodlett champions, "even when taken between teeth." *Twice Shy* understands the difficulty in this vulnerability, but also doesn't shy away from its necessity ("the unfinished...both burden and ballast"). This is a writer to join hands with, because she reaches out honestly, generously. Thank goodness for Luiza Flynn-Goodlett.

– **MIAH JEFFRA**, author of
The First Church of What's Happening

Twice Shy

Luiza Flynn-Goodlett

NOMADIC PRESS

OAKLAND
111 FAIRMOUNT AVENUE
OAKLAND, CA 94611

BROOKLYN
475 KENT AVENUE #302
BROOKLYN, NY 11249

WWW.NOMADICPRESS.ORG

MASTHEAD

FOUNDING AND MANAGING EDITOR
J. K. FOWLER

ASSOCIATE EDITOR
MICHAELA MULLIN

DESIGN
J. K. FOWLER

MISSION STATEMENT

Nomadic Press is a 501 (C)(3) not-for-profit organization that supports the works of emerging and established writers and artists. Through publications (including translations) and performances, Nomadic Press aims to build community among artists and across disciplines.

SUBMISSIONS

Nomadic Press wholeheartedly accepts unsolicited book manuscripts. To submit your work, please visit www.nomadicpress.org/submissions

DISTRIBUTION

Orders by trade bookstores and wholesalers:
Small Press Distribution,
1341 Seventh Street
Berkeley, CA 94701
spd@spdbooks.org
(510) 524-1668 / (800) 869-7553

Twice Shy
© 2020 by Luiza Flynn-Goodlett

This book was made possible by a loving community of chosen family and friends, old and new.

For author questions or to book a reading at your bookstore, university/school, or alternative establishment, please send an email to info@nomadicpress.org.

Cover artwork and author portrait by Arthur Johnstone

Published by Nomadic Press, 111 Fairmount Avenue, Oakland, CA 94611

First printing, 2020

Printed in the United States of America

LIBRARY OF CONGRESS CATALOGING-IN-PUBLICATION DATA

Flynn-Goodlett, Luiza 1984 –
Title: *Twice Shy*
P. CM.
Summary: *Twice Shy* by Luiza Flynn-Goodlett reflects the many faces of violence—in our experiences, our relationships, and our society—but it then asks us to turn toward the light, to heal the fractured self. This collection is a roadmap to a place of radical tenderness.

[1. POETRY/VIOLENCE. 2. POETRY/RESILIENCE. 3. AMERICAN GENERAL.] I. III. TITLE.

LIBRARY OF CONGRESS CONTROL NUMBER: 2019957651

ISBN: 978-1-7344377-3-7

Twice
Shy

Luiza Flynn-Goodlett

**NOMADIC
PRESS**

CONTENTS

INTRODUCTION

1   THE SUBLIME BEFORE
    (IS SOMEONE'S AFTER)

2   TENDERIZERS

3   THREE CHOICES

4   BEFORE BABEL

5   UNLUCKY PENNY

6   HE SAYS/SHE SAYS

7   AGAINST FORGIVENESS

8   TO PENCE

9   FACTS OF LIFE

10 THINK WELL OF US

11 GREENBOTTLE

12 THE WORST

13 *I SURVIVED*

14 I HATE A POEM WITH
    POEM IN IT

15 NOTICERS

16 MIRACLE FISH

17 DARKLING

18 MEMORY LOSS

19   HOW TO TELL

21   SEVEN YEARS AFTER

22   ON WANTING TO LIVE

23   SOFT TEACHERS

24   (THE SUBLIME BEFORE)
       IS SOMEONE'S AFTER

CLASSROOM GUIDE

INTRODUCTION

After the 2016 election, I began to see violence—systemic, environmental, intergenerational, sexual, self-inflicted—everywhere. Violence had not only touched me, but everyone I loved, and even the natural world that was my sanctuary. In many ways, I was helpless against it. I came to recognize that I would always exist alongside violence as long as I lived in a society that worships brutality, just as the violence I experienced will always live inside me, manifesting in triggers and memory loss. But I could reject violence's attempts to shape me in its image—I could instead become softer, kinder, more patient, more loving. *Twice Shy* represents this journey toward a state of radical tenderness.

THE SUBLIME BEFORE (IS SOMEONE'S AFTER)

Red-throated hummingbirds spar above

the magnolia. Upwind, something grilled.

The dogs are still alive, yap at whitetail in

the cornfield. The rooster hasn't chased us

down the driveway, so no one got fed up,

loaded the shotgun. Father's heart doesn't

yet float on a pillow of fat. The miscarriage

is years off. Summers, we bleach hair with

lemon, are warm as gold on skin, haven't

glimpsed the shapes we'll be hammered in.

TENDERIZERS

Some crack ribcages to
lift the lace of fat, weave
arteries, bypass blocks.
Third time's the charm,

he jokes, chest a mess
of staples. It's the family
affliction—what's supple
calcifies, and soon, can't

wake us. At least, that's
how grandpa went, how
we tell it. The truth is, he
courted it—drew whiskey

baths, wreathed in smoke.
And I do much the same—
array clots to spasm, cold
paddles to shock me back.

THREE CHOICES

First, left she who sowed
fields with salt. Crammed

clothes in trash bags, bolted.
Second, this sea-glass coast,

moss on redwoods. Lastly,
a different woman—books

unpacked onto my shelves.
These three sketch Polaris,

point due north. But when
feverish, babbling into her

neck, it's clear that I moved
my pieces without glancing

at the board—ran to check
the mail as a plane crashed,

roof ablaze. I wasn't spared.
Didn't learn a thing. Will

stumble through the next
doorway, grope for a light.

BEFORE BABEL

As water over rocks, infant's wail, we rang
with clarity, our gratitude for being created

still a sweet, formless taffy. Leave it to Him
to take it wrong. He wanted us as flowers

seeking sun, knees sore from stone. But we
neared Him with every moan, and so, made

an offering of what in us was most alive—its
thrust direct, reaching to touch. The rest is

known. Each cursed with her own, singular
language, we roam the wilds of confusion.

UNLUCKY PENNY

I know, I told you to flick it into the gutter
and turn on your heel, but lied, stowed it in

my purse's depths. I cup its glint, but it's too
humble to grant passage, entice a ferryman.

No, I'll need a coin that covers my eyes, large
enough to choke. Barring that, the pill stash

in the sock drawer will probably suffice. Abe
frowns in his cameo, drunk on superiority,

but I'm still stuck at a dead end, flipping this
cent-piece, hoping, once, it comes down tails.

HE SAYS/SHE SAYS

But, she doesn't, until
he drowns in a hospital,
begging seven children's

forgiveness. Where are
the fists that sparked, set
them burning? Tongues

of flame that licked down
her throat? Underground.
His Centralia smolders—

exhales noxious vapor,
opens sinkholes to itself.
Decades later, plucking

cinders from her hair, she
remembers the night he
stopped. Mother tucked

her in instead, said, *You're
a big girl now*. And, for
better or worse, she was.

AGAINST FORGIVENESS

You're told it's honey, sweet
on the tongue, a poultice for
what in you hasn't stopped

screaming. Perhaps. Others
lived through what you did,
stand upright. He has likely

forgotten too, conflated you
with another pair of ruined
tights, muddy saddle shoes.

Then why insist on calling
down this well that flings
your voice back, distorted

and faint? It's just that here,
treading water, is the child
you were, skin he unzipped

you from. Sole visitor, you
can't leave her where she was
flung ages ago. She may find

handholds in moss, climb
skyward, or drown gagging,
but you must sit, witness it.

TO PENCE

It works just as you imagine,
involves as much buffoonery,

gymnastics, pauses to readjust,
switch hands. You're right, we
have at least one pair of cuffs,

varieties of lube, and get lonely,
can be found against bathroom

walls between ringlets of graffiti.
We too feared being alone with
a woman, once found her hair tie

on the rug, blond caught in metal,
saved it. We've stood at S/M-club

snack tables, tugging Twizzlers
with our teeth, yet can't count
the times we felt a body open to

pleasure, those noises it makes
like nothing you've ever heard.

FACTS OF LIFE

Death seems the most salient,
a Vantablack that flattens this
lush riot into two dimensions,

spaghettifies approaching days,
maroons us in the anxious *now*.
And, worse, we can't know how

tightly our watch was wound,
at what moment its whiskers
will no longer tickle, whole

mechanism stutter to a stop,
only that it must. How could
some be accorded one breath,

others a century of inhalations?
It's certainly not merit-based,
as any skinflint shivering his

dotage away can attest; eldest,
taken by fever, and youngest
(*a fag*), he's not speaking to.

Still, a certain quality of light
sneaks in sometimes, strokes
his jaw with bright fingers.

THINK WELL OF US

Though we rats fled this ship
before it sank, what little time
we had we spent gnawing rinds,

squealing. And, yes, we saw
it coming, closets of unworn
winter clothes, a bonanza for

moths. Even so, woke at noon,
ate oranges by the bagful. Can
you forgive failures, operatic

at this distance—Salton Sea
gone desert, fire ants lacing
floodwater with red ribbon.

Heat-buckled concrete tripped
us, but we caught ourselves,
kissed the top of your head in

the carrier. I know, we can't
leave you here. But we will.

GREENBOTTLE

Princeling's gilt button, nearly knuckle-sized, you

dodge the swatter, alight just out of reach. You're

forensics' friend, first to colonize the corpse, yet,

given a living host, turn nurse, polish off diseased

tissue. What in us festered, turned rancid? Gold

filling in ash, you keep mum, gleam of the grave.

We'll mistake the flutter for blood's thrum, when

the ferryman docks, fumble you into his palm.

THE WORST

I've spent a lifetime bent to its whisper—
buckling seat belts, checking deadbolts—
a temple scribe made to minister among

heretics streaking by on motorcycles,
scarves trailing. But, at night, converts
come—the pregnant, the pilots, those

whose fathers are newly forgetful—
array on rugs to fill lamps with fear,
which burns hotter than oil, brighter

than the match hope keeps striking,
even though the shadows capering on
my walls are lies, hardly ever arrive.

I SURVIVED

Never pick up hitchhikers, help
a man on crutches load his van.

Heed gut feelings, or else, mimic
intimacy, shield your skull, play

dead after the second shot. Take
deep breaths before being forced

underwater. Hands hacked off to
delay ID, scale the embankment,

flag a passing car. Tell everyone,
just loved ones, or no one since

you hydroplaned over it, don't
recall a thing, or do, but only

his fly popping undone, sky
searing blue beyond the trees,

the taste of rope. No one wants
to hear how time's gooey; even

now, if someone comes up from
behind, walks a certain way, you

fall back, can barely be reached—
faces haloed, streetlights in fog—

and, all the time, carry survival,
necessary and half-forgotten as

tampons at the bottom of a purse,
saying you've bled, still bleed, live.

I HATE A POEM WITH *POEM* IN IT

It's a southern tic—we only tell truth
to a screen door, swinging closed; never
simply *ask*, instead say, *Would you care*

for potatoes? wait for someone to return
the favor; despite shearling and Doc
Martens, I was sure nobody knew I'd

been playing scales along the neighbor
girl's thighs; mother only told us after
surgery, once it went well; even when

they heard I wasn't the first child he'd
pulled into those woods, no one was
called—we dissemblers, muddled as

the mint in a julep, erect monuments
to history we can't face, won't just say,
Yep, it's a poem, *now, pass the potatoes.*

NOTICERS

Always odd, they sit to the side
while soccer balls arc into nets,

others dive after, confetti grass.
They beat erasers to clouds, hone

noticing against skin's whetstone,
the perpetual blush, a small price

to pay, might even notice you—
penny on gray concrete—polish

you with a glance. Most can't
abide their breath of southern

summer, eyes wonder-wide, but
the few who follow these gravel

roads barefoot find honeysuckle,
deer breaking from briars, the dirt

path to a waterfall that you'd never
notice, if they hadn't pointed it out.

MIRACLE FISH

Only five-and-dime purchase possible
with change from our Buick's backseat,
I shook you free and you floated, candy-

red, into my palm. Wafer of wisdom,
you were supposed to move in response
to my inquiries, but baffled with words

(*jealousy, indifference, fickle*) I'd never
encountered. *Love's* flash of both head
and tail was most elusive. A full-body

curl was all you'd offer. A fair mimic at
least, I held that pose for years until, fins
tongued warm, I began, at last, to dance.

DARKLING

Bloody bowling ball, I come
out bald and bawling, won't
latch. When my pate fuzzes,
white as a geezer's, I speak—

too early, with a changeling's
charm. Kindergarten's sticky
mitts soon stain strands dun.
For decades, I flail in the fairy

ring—bleach it bone, streak it
rainbow, forget its true weight—
clapper ringing my skull's bell.
Only now, loam-black riven by

gray, do I return to it. As Silly
Putty pressed to newsprint, it
lapped a lifetime of dark, rests
the coiled crown at my brow.

MEMORY LOSS

Siblings testify to swaddling blanket

texture as I struggle to name cousins,

huge swaths redacted by the hand that

shoved a small head toward his zipper.

It unravels—shoes wet from the stream,

lost hair ribbon, child under her desk

thinking of geodes, how she hammered

until their jeweled insides showed—into

the tangle from which I tug this thread,

too frayed to pass through my empty eye.

HOW TO TELL

When put plainly, its obscene,

artless gestures—drunk sisters

in a hammer fight—reduce us

to baser matter, body against

body, sully those who handle

it, although we never sought

it, even while it's happening,

can hardly believe it, though,

being girls, we'd prepared since

birth, and so say, *Take anything*

you want. We'll never know what

he wanted, other than a clump

of hair. You back away. Heard

enough? So, how to *tell* without

handing over this wet weight

like an empty overcoat? Then,

as you finger buttons, rummage

through pockets, explain, this is

nothing. We haven't even begun.

SEVEN YEARS AFTER

I know, you believe in
nothing, so when you

step off the fire escape,
fall into nothing, never

bloody the courtyard's
snowdrifts. Nobody

screams, rushes down
to slick dress red. But,

as of today, I'm the older
one, and can't say there's

much to recommend it,
just more living, which

you'd already tried. Yet,
you were wrong, aren't

nothing—the atoms you
animated reapportioned

to whitecaps, peaches,
ice sweating in whiskey—

an escape was impossible
from the start. It all keeps

going, takes you along for
the ride. With us. Always.

ON WANTING TO LIVE

The unfinished—teetering books

at bedside, cat mewing as her can

opens—is both burden and ballast.

Knife to oyster, it pries. The toddler

who palms a stove's red eye, fingers

sticking; doe who darts out before

a truck; jumper clawing air beneath

the Golden Gate—you're a glutton

for everything, even punishment.

SOFT TEACHERS

In a season of snares and hounds,
hares are nothing more than dun

flashes in foliage. Hunters hunger
as the four-footed tend burrows

of blind babies. These prophets
are as you were once—nuzzling,

barely formed. Let leaves crunch
above, dogs bark without a shiver.

Stay prey—fur glossy, eyes bright—
even when taken between teeth.

(THE SUBLIME BEFORE)
IS SOMEONE'S AFTER

Both fathers grabbed them by the throat.

One uncle, drunk, drove off a bridge. Her

mother, pregnant nine times, had seven

children; his was an icicle chain-smoking

on the porch. Her pelvis, crushed under

a semi, tilted the cervical cap, so the first

of us was a *happy accident*. How remarkable

then, the veil—Queen Anne's lace, deer-cut

paths in the woods, periwinkles adorning

creek beds—drawn over all that. We wear

it still, stir delicate stitches with breath.

CLASSROOM GUIDE

Twice Shy is an unsparing exploration of violence in its varied manifestations and aftermaths. The collection grapples with how bystanders and even loved ones are deputized to ignore or minimize violence in "He Says/She Says," while survivors are gaslit into silence. Luiza Flynn-Goodlett breaks that silence with poems like "Against Forgiveness," connecting individual traumas to larger systems of power and oppression that subject people of marginalized genders to ongoing brutality.

Flynn-Goodlett locates healing in exactly the aspects of herself that are most pathologized and derided. When reclaimed, they become founts of strength, evidenced by gritty resilience in "I Survived," and rejection of dominant narratives of queer identity in "To Pence." There's palpable fearlessness in poems like "How to Tell," which manifests in determination to speak truth, even to an indifferent or hostile audience.

Flynn-Goodlett also recognizes how untenable living often feels in our inherently violent society. She reflects on her own suicidal ideation in "Unlucky Penny," and commemorates the anniversary of a friend's suicide in "Seven Years." In this context, healing comes in fits and starts. It necessitates honoring parts of the self that may never be recovered ("Memory Loss"), while treating what remains with tenderness, as in "Soft Teachers," which exhorts the reader to "Stay prey—fur glossy, eyes bright— / even when taken between teeth."

DISCUSSION QUESTIONS

1. Flynn-Goodlett frequently uses colloquial phrases—such as "Facts of Life," "Think Well of Us," or "Twice Shy"—as jumping-off places. How do her poems highlight or lend different meanings to these phrases? What are some common phrases that you find interesting or poetic?

2. Many of Flynn-Goodlett's poems feature natural elements, settings, and animals. How does she use the natural world to contrast human society? Does the speaker align herself more with nature or with people—why?

3. In "To Pence," Flynn-Goodlett attempts to refute homophobic stereotypes by contrasting them against her lived experiences. This poem also directly addresses the Vice President. Are there are public figures whose stances on aspects of your identity are untrue and/or hateful? What might you want to

tell them about who you really are?

4. Flynn-Goodlett situates herself in a familial lineage in poems like "'Tenderizers.'" What are some words that the speaker might associate with family? Are those words a mix of negative and positive? If so, why do you think that is?

5. *Twice Shy* is bookended by two poems with very similar titles: "The Sublime Before (Is Someone's After)" and "(The Sublime Before) Is Someone's After." How do you think these poems are related? Has the speaker learned something between the two poems? If so, what?

ACKNOWLEDGEMENTS

Thank you to the following publications for permission to reprint some of the poems that appear in this chapbook: "I Hate a Poem with *Poem* In It," *Booth;* "Think Well of Us," Broadsided Press; "Three Choices," *The Pinch;* "(The Sublime Before) Is Someone's After," *Puerto del Sol*; "The Sublime Before (Is Someone's After)," *Quarterly West*; "Greenbottle," *RHINO*; "Against Forgiveness," "How To Tell," The Rumpus; "Seven Years After," *Salamander*; and "To Pence, He Says/She Says, I Survived," *South Dakota Review*

LUIZA FLYNN-GOODLETT is the author of the
forthcoming collection *Look Alive*, winner of the 2019 Cowles
Poetry Book Prize from Southeast Missouri State University
Press, along with six chapbooks, most recently *Tender Age*,
winner of the 2019 Headmistress Press Charlotte Mew chapbook
contest, and *Shadow Box*, winner of the 2019 Madhouse Press
Editor's Prize. Her poetry can be found in *Third Coast*, *Pleiades*,
The Journal, *The Common*, and elsewhere. She serves as editor-
in-chief of *Foglifter* and lives in sunny Oakland, California.